THE MAGIC WORLD

American Indian Songs and Poems

THE MAGIC WORLD

American Indian Songs and Poems

SELECTED AND EDITED
WITH AN INTRODUCTION BY
WILLIAM BRANDON

William Morrow & Company, Inc.
New York
1971

Heleney

3   4   5   75   74   73   72

Acknowledgments of gratitude can not reach or for the most part even name the generations of singers and storytellers who created these songs and poems. Consequently the anonymous contributors' share of the royalties from this book will go, on behalf of these unknown poets, to the Diné Biólta Association, a Navajo organization concerned with bilingual education, as a gesture of encouragement for educational programs in the languages that produced this literature.

I want to express special thanks to the Southwest Museum, the Bancroft Library, and the Henry E. Huntington Library, all of California, for their many courtesies and kindnesses, and to the following individuals and publishers for permission to publish copyrighted material:

The American Folklore Society, Inc., for a selection from Frank G. Speck, "Malecite Tales," in *Journal of American Folk-Lore,* Vol. 30, No. 108, 1917.

Paul Bernal, Taos Pueblo, N.M., for "The Sacred Lands of the Blue Lake Forest."

Editorial Porrua, S.A., for a selection from Angel María Garibay K., *Poesía Náhuatl,* México, 1964.

Estate of Knud Rasmussen, for selections from *The Intellectual Culture of the Iglulik Eskimos,* Copenhagen, 1929.

Estate of Paul A. W. Wallace, for selections from *The White Roots of Peace,* Philadelphia, 1946.

Houghton Mifflin Co., for a selection from Dane and Mary Roberts Coolidge, *The Navaho Indians,* Boston, 1930.

Museum of Navaho Ceremonial Art, Inc., Santa Fe, New Mexico, for a selection from the *Museum of Navaho Ceremonial Art Bulletin No. 4* (1946).

Museum of the American Indian, Heye Foundation, for selections from *Frances Densmore and American Indian Music,* New York, 1968.

Oklahoma Historical Society, for permission to reprint an original document published by the Society in the *Chronicles of Oklahoma,* Vol. 12 (September, 1934).

Princeton University Press, for excerpts from *Beautyway,* recorded and translated by Father Berard Haile, ed. by Leland C. Wyman, Bollingen Series LIII, published by Princeton University Press (copyright © 1957 by Bollingen Foundation).

Rough Rock Demonstration School's *Rough Rock News,* Chinle, Arizona, for "Concerning Wisdom" by Dan Yazzie.

School of American Research, Santa Fe, N.M., for excerpts from Book II of *General History of The Things of New Spain: The Florentine Codex,* printed by permission of the copyright holder, the School of American Research, Santa Fe, N.M.

Mrs. Ailes Spinden, for a selection from Herbert J. Spinden, *Songs of the Tewa,* New York, 1933.

Southwest Museum, Los Angeles, California, for excerpts from Frances Densmore, *Music of the Santo Domingo Pueblo, New Mexico, Southwest Museum Paper No. 12.*

University of Oklahoma Press, for a selection from *The Aztecs: People of the Sun,* by Alfonso Caso, translated by Lowell Dunham. Copyright 1958 by the University of Oklahoma Press.

Syracuse University Press, for selections from *Parker on the Iroquois: Iroquois Uses of Maize and Other Food Plants; The Code of Handsome Lake, the Seneca Prophet; The Constitution of the Five Nations;* by Arthur C. Parker; William N. Fenton, editor. Syracuse University Press, 1968.

CONTENTS

· vii ·

INTRODUCTION

The poems can speak for themselves. They are presented here not as ethnological data but strictly as literature. There should be no more need to talk about the "cultures" of the various American Indian groups than to preface Catullus with a discourse on ancient Rome.

They come originally from countless generations of poets and singers of the American Indian world, a world devoted to the mystery of poetry; they are found in writing in collections of legends, rituals, songs, tales, poems, myth cycles, gathered from end to end of the hemisphere by explorers, soldiers, teachers, native American scribes and chroniclers, missionaries, traders, vagabonds, ethnographers, over the past four and a half centuries. The sheer quantity of such poetry is staggering. Several hundred volumes are listed at the end of this book; there are many hundreds more, and still more in languages other than English, particularly in Spanish.

Dr. Washington Matthews, in the Navajo country in the 1880's, found chants, prayers, song-cycles "so numerous that one can never hope to collect them all." Multivolume collections have been made from tiny Indian communities with populations of only a few hundred persons, as among the Malecite people of the Maine-New Brunswick border or in some of New Mexico's Pueblo villages—where additional volumes still remain in only oral circulation. Maya literature, said Bishop Landa of Yucatan writing in the 1560's, included history, science, lives of great men, astronomy, astrology, prophecy, theology, ritual, legends, fables, medicine, grammar, "certain songs in meter" and "comedies for the pleasure of the public." Bishop Landa piously burned all this ("which," he wrote, "the Indians regretted to an amazing degree and which caused them great anguish") so that nothing remains except remembered fragments, lovely, tattered, hopelessly garbled ("With rivers of tears we mourned our sacred writings among the delicate flowers of sorrow," wrote an unknown Maya poet); but even these scraps and remnants fill some thousands of pages.

The religious and artistic preoccupation of the Indian world went far beyond anything in the European/American experience. Life was a mystical adventure, and making up songs and singing them its most important business. Much of this was a wholly religious business, in which poetry (the great universal hypnotic, the all-time-great mind-altering drug) transformed the soul to an awareness of the beauty and holiness of—in Hölderlin's phrase—the "permanent real"; but much of it was only for fun and entertainment, in which poetry added the joyous dimension of fantasy for which, seemingly, the day-to-day American Indian life was lived.

It was a life that appeared (to European eyes) to consist overwhelmingly of play taken seriously. If the Pawnees had operated a General Motors, each worker would have had his time-clock-punching song, his assembly-line song, and so on, and the management would have been at least as attentive to the songs as to the rate of production, probably more so.

The Indian world was, and is, a world immensely alien to European tradition, a world more alien, really, than we can even yet quite realize. Its literature does give us insights into this alienness, and the literature has been most often studied for this exclusive purpose, that is, as technical data that may serve in some special way to inform us of this marvelously foreign world.

But it is infinitely more than scientific data. It contains pages as beautiful, as meaningful, as any of the world's great literatures, and (in spite of its alien source) as immediate and moving to any reader as are the best pages from any other great literature. Some of our most honored masterpieces, such as the works of Homer, have descended from the same conditions that apply to most American Indian literature: oral tradition, translation, uncertain authorship. Certainly a work of art loses nothing by springing from anonymous hands. It should even gain, by fixing attention on the poem rather than the poet.

But the emphasis on a scientific point of view has left a legacy of feeling, especially in quarters anxious to cultivate a scientific air, that this poetry can not be taken seriously as poetry, being mere magic formulae chanted by the primitive hunter for success in his primitive endeavors. Some of it is indeed rigidly constructed of religion in action, as is some of ours (e.g., the Twenty-third Psalm or the Song of Solomon or the *sutras* of Bodhidharma), and all of it indeed came out of a magic world, if magic, like true poetry, is simply that which can not quite be understood in prose.

But the question of the "seriousness" of this literature needs somewhat more of an answer. It was taken seriously as literature in the early centuries of Europe's acquaintance with the New World by such Europeans as the essayist Montaigne, but as the Indian world, the "orchidean" New World as William Carlos Williams termed it, was smashed and splintered and its people reduced to paupers and therefore objects of contempt for our businessman's society, its literature likewise lost any respectably serious status. And yet the world it sang, the world of natural truth and beauty and of men free from tyranny and toil, exercised from the beginning a most serious influence on the course of literature and life in Europe and later in America. Montaigne's utopian view of this New World and its golden freedom was used, word for word, by Shakespeare for Gonzalo's speech on the ideal commonwealth in *The Tempest;* the missionary Jean Baptiste Dutertre's rhapsodic report on this world of freedom and equality, published in the mid-seventeenth century, was used line for line by Rousseau in his revolutionary remarks a hundred years later; Lewis Henry Morgan's vision of the League of the Iroquois, published in the mid-nineteenth century, was used by Marx and Engels in presenting their vision of a socialist world of the future. These witnesses would seem to testify to seriousness enough, as far as content is concerned.

Of techniques, artistic skills, a further word: Some of the pages in this book are relics from a past now dead, some are living creations of an endless present constantly absorbing an endless past; but certain of the literary techniques may have been practiced more or less unchanged throughout centuries, perhaps throughout millennia in such relatively changeless lands as Indian California, leading to an extraordinary virtuosity, as in this opening of a Hupa tale from northern California:

A modest woman lived there who seldom went out of her house. One day as she was sitting working on her baskets a ray of sunlight fell on her without cause. What is going to happen? she thought. . . .

Characterization, narrative interest, atmosphere ("a ray of sunlight fell on her *without cause*") are here compressed into an introductory chord that even Chekov could envy. In such cases of ultravirtuosity, ultrasophistication, we find ourselves plunged into a most literary of literatures: the *word* above all, the word become truly magical not only by its meaning but also by its artful manipulation.

Dealt with as data, the language of this literature has been handled as gingerly as fingerprints at the scene of the crime. The linguistic anthropologists have been interested in precision not poetry, in what the word denotes not what it connotes, as Herbert J. Spinden remarked a generation ago.

I have used the word with the same freedom with the word that I would use with Sappho or Gottschalk or any poetry in translation. My sole aim has been to remember that these are living words, not quaint transliterations from an inaccessibly "primitive" world. My only criterion has been, do the lines feel good, moving? I have tried to pay no attention whatsoever to the value of a given piece as ethnological information, or for that matter to its religious or mystical or historical significance. I have tried to approach each line exactly as I might approach a line of Sappho's, only as literature. For a simplest example: the problem of the matter of repetition, repetition being the common denominator of much Indian poetry. Some images otherwise beautiful to us are buried all but out of sight in repetition, perhaps each line being repeated as many as half a dozen times. Our ears can get the same effect of hypnotic repetition with considerably less actual repeating. Or in some cases a suggestion of ritual might be conveyed in English by three repetitions—our mystic number—rather than the four or five or six or seven called for by the original ritual directions. In the buffalo songs, for instance, it would not only be wearisome to follow faithfully all the magic numbers, but we might also, who knows, materialize a buffalo. We don't really want the buffalo. We only want the feeling of the earnest repetition, the feeling of the hypnosis, of the marvelous emerging, the feeling of the magic. All that we want from any of it is the feeling of its poetry. Let the ethnologists keep its "science" and the oncoming generations of Indian poets its mystery.

William Brandon

MONTEREY, CALIFORNIA

THE MAGIC WORLD

American Indian Songs and Poems

A MODOC SINGER: *Introduction*

I
the song
I walk here

From a translation in A. L. Kroeber, *Handbook of California Indians. Bureau of American Ethnology Bulletin 78,* Washington, D.C., 1925.

NAHUATL: *Aztec Song*

we only came to sleep
we only came to dream
it is not true
no it is not true
that we came to live on the earth

we are changed into the grass of springtime
our hearts will grow green again
and they will open their petals
but our body is like a rose tree
              it puts forth flowers and then withers

From Antonio Peñafiel, MS Colección de Cantares
Mexicanos, National Library of Mexico, Folio 17; re-
printed here from *The Aztecs: People of the Sun,* by
Alfonso Caso, translated by Lowell Dunham, Copy-
right 1958 by the University of Oklahoma Press.

MAYA HYMN: *A Fragment*

maker
of all created things
who gives breath and thought

(she who gives birth to the children)
(he who watches over the happiness of the people
the happiness of the human race)

the wise man
who meditates
on the goodness
of all that exists
in the sky
in the earth
in the lakes
and in
the sea. . . .

"A Hymn to the Creator and the Maker, the Mother
and Father of Life," from the *Popol Vuh,* translated
by Sylvanus Griswold Morley, Norman, Okla., 1950.

TUPI: *Love-charm Songs*

I
You magic power in the skies
who love the rains
make it so that he
no matter how many women he has
will think them all ugly
make him remember me
remember me
this afternoon
when the sun goes to the west

II
New moon
new moon
here I am in your presence
make it so
that only I
may occupy his heart

Altered slightly from Couto de Magalães, *O Selvagem,*
Rio de Janeiro, 1876.

"The Tupi . . . have long had a reputation for
poetic compositions especially among the French. This
may date from 1550 when a large band of Tupi In-
dians took part in a festival at Rouen. In 1557 Jean
de Lery recorded during a voyage in Brazil several
fragments of songs which had impressed him deeply.
Much later the eminent Montaigne was provided with
a few examples of Tupi songs by a man who had spent
several years among these Indians, and was moved to
declare that the verses were worthy of Anacreon."——
Herbert J. Spinden, 1933.

Among the Tupian peoples in the Amazon drain-
age were some of the most uproarious cannibals on
earth.

NAHUATL: *Flower Song*

(TO BEGIN TO THE RHYTHM *QUITITI, QUI-
TITI, QUITI TOCOTO, TOCOTI, TOCOTO, TO-
COTI* AND THEN TO TURN AGAIN AND RE-
PEAT)

Let me pluck flowers let me see them let me gather intoxicating
  flowers
the flowers are ready many colored varied in color
ready for our enjoyment

The flowers are here in this secluded place ready here
in this spot of fragrant flowers
here in this spot many sorts of flowers are as if poured on the earth
scattered about this spot

   (let the drum be ready for the dance)

I the singer take and pour down before you from my soul
the beautiful poyomatl
  (the narcotic rose, to be mixed with tobacco and smoked)
not to be painted
and other flowers

let us rejoice
while I alone within my soul disclose the songs of flowers
and scatter them abroad in the place of flowers

I shall leave my songs
in order that I may mingle them with the flowers of my heart
with the children and the great men (still to come, still to be
  born)

I weep as I see that I must leave the earth
and leave my flowers my songs

that the day will come
when these flowers of my heart
even these also
will become vain and useless

Adapted from Daniel G. Brinton, *Ancient Nahuatl Poetry*, Philadelphia, 1877.

NAHUATL: *From the Aztec Ceremonial Calendar*

In the rites of the first month they slew many children
they sacrificed them in different holy places upon the mountain
       tops
tearing from them their hearts in
honor of the gods of water
    so that these might then give rain

The children were decked in rich finery when they were taken to
       to be killed
they were carried in litters upon the shoulders of the people
the litters went adorned with feathers and flowers and
    the priests danced before
    playing musical instruments
    dancing and singing

If the children wept and shed tears those
who carried them (carried them to be slain) rejoiced
    for this was an omen there would be much rain that year

Also in this month they slew many captives in this same honor
in honor of these same gods of water

The owners of the captives to be slain in the second month
took their slaves to the temple where they were to be slain
they took them by the hair
up the steps of the pyramid dragging them by the hair
up to the sacrificial stone
and tore off the hair of the crowns of the captives' heads
to keep as a relic

On the feast of the third month were offered the first blossoms of
    flowers
of the flowers then blooming earliest in the year

Before these had been offered
none dared smell a flower

At the feast of the fourth month they placed reeds
reeds at the doors of the houses
and sprinkled them with blood from their ears or
from the calves of their legs

And the rich set up in their houses branches and
set forth branches and flowers for the gods

The feast of the fifth month was the most important of all
like the feast of Easter
and indeed it fell near the time of Easter

This was the feast of Tezcatlipoca
when they slew the most comely youth who had lived for one year
as the god

To celebrate the feast of the sixth month
priests went for reeds to the waters of Temilco
where reeds grew large and handsome
and brought them to adorn the pyramids

During this journey of the priests all wayfarers hid themselves
no one appeared in sight
for fear of the priests and their sacred journey

On this same feast they slew captives and other slaves
arrayed in the ornaments of the god Tlaloc

In the feast of the seventh month was slain the woman
who was the likeness of the goddess called Uixtociuatl
(Tlaloc's elder sister)

Women
old women
young women
girls
sang and danced
wearing garlands and holding flowers

Dancing they took captives to the Pyramid of Tlaloc
where the priests slew first the captives and then the woman
the woman in the likeness of the goddess

In the eighth month they slew a woman in honor of
the goddess of tender maize
and eight days before this all men and women
young and old
feasted and danced

they joined hands or embraced
and danced in rhythm

The ninth month was the feast of the god of war

all feasted on fowls and dogs and tamales

all the statues of the gods were decorated with
flowers
flowers were offered
and dancing

On the tenth month was the feast to the god of fire
when were cast into fire alive

many slaves bound hand and foot
 (first a powder was thrown into their faces that dulled
 their senses that they might lose their sense of feeling
 and not suffer so greatly)
then while still alive
they were taken forth out of the fire
and their hearts torn out before the god of fire

In the eleventh month they danced in silence
and slew in perfect silence a woman representing the goddess
called Our Grandmother

In the twelfth month the young men and boys
strewed boughs on the altars
and washed the feet of the god

The thirteenth month was in honor of the high mountains
when offerings of dough and tamales were made
and four women and one man were slain to the mountains

The fourteenth month was celebrated by the making of
darts and arrows both for war and for hunting

captives bound like deer were slain

in these days no man might lie with his wife

In the fifteenth month slaves decked in paper ornaments
were sacrificed with music and dancing to
the god of war

The sixteenth month was the month of rain and
the priests of the Tlalocs offered incense and
made images of paper with squash seeds for teeth and beans for
　　　eyes
and slew these images in sacrifice

The seventeenth month was the feast of Our Mother
when a woman representing the goddess Our Mother was slain
and the priest carried her head by its hair in his right hand
and led with it the movements of the dance

The eighteenth month celebrated the god of fire
an image was made in his honor made with great artifice
an image which appeared to throw off flames of its own accord

every four years at this feast they slew slaves and captives
in the honor of this god

and at this feast they pierced the ears of all the children
born in those years
and gave them godfathers and godmothers

The five remaining days of the year were days
of ill fortune
unlucky days

Of the movable feasts one was held in honor of the sun
when incense and quail were offered and
captives slain at noon

in another painters and seamstresses fasted and offered incense
that they might paint well and weave well

in another the people sang and played and drank to the gods of
        wine
and in another gifts were made to warriors and singers
and in another offerings of perfumes to the god of the winds
and in another quail and perfumes to the great god Tezcatlipoca
and in another those condemned to death for some crime were
        slain
in honor of women who died in first childbed
and in another merchants celebrated trade
and in others ornaments of the gods were cleaned
children were protected
watersellers and fishermen honored the goddess of water
new births were celebrated good fortune prayed for
and in another a dance was enacted in which the people assumed
the forms or characters of various birds and animals

Adapted from Book II of Fray Bernardino de Sahagun, *General History of the Things of New Spain;* the *Florentine Codex,* translated by Charles E. Dibble and Arthur J. O. Anderson, Santa Fe, 1950 ff.

NAHUATL: *The Feast of the Great God Tezcatlipoca*

In the fifth month was the great feast
the feast of Tezcatlipoca

At this feast died the youth the fair
youth the young man without
blemish
who for one year had lived as the god

For he who was chosen
from among the most select of captives
from among say the ten most fair of body and good
to look upon
he who was chosen to be the god
was slain on this day

And on this same day a new impersonator of the god
who again would live for one year
was offered to the people

The youth chosen was of radiant countenance
of good understanding
quick and clean of body
                    slender like a reed
                    lean and well built as a cane
                    neither corpulent nor small
                    nor overly tall
                            (for of one too tall the women said
                            Headnodder
                            Star-hands)

He who was chosen was entirely without defect
                    smooth as a pebble or carved wood

or a tomato
       hair long and straight
       skin without spot

       no scabs or boils or
       warts
       nor large headed nor with the back
       of the head too large nor the head
       shaped like a carrying-net
       nor with the head too broad or
       too square nor
       bald nor with the forehead
       bulbous nor with the eyelids
       swollen nor the eyes
       bulging

       nor with any disfigurement

                 nor with
       cleft chin or gross face or
       a face downcast

       or flat nosed or
       with nostrils too wide

                 nor a
       nose bent or twisted but a nose
       straight and well placed

       nor with lips thick or gross
       or shaped like bowls

       nor with a tongue that stammered
       or talked as if pierced for a ring

       nor one who spoke a barbarous

language
or spoke thickly or
lisped
or was dumb

nor buck-toothed large-
toothed fang-toothed yellow-
toothed or with teeth
black or decayed but with
teeth like seashells
in perfect order

neither with scarred eyes
nor squinting
nor small-eyed seed-
eyed angry-eyed sunken-
eyed

nor scarred about the neck
or double-chinned or with
protruding ears or long ears

nor long necked

or hunchbacked or maimed
in any way

and not fat-fingered or
fat-bellied

                              nor of
pushed-out navel or ax-

shaped buttocks nor of
flabby buttocks or
thighs

and not cringing

He who was thus without flaw
with no defects no
blemishes no moles no
scars or wrinkles on his body

he then was taught to play the flute
taught music and graces
taught to smoke gracefully the pipe
taught to carry gracefully flowers and
enjoy gracefully their scent

also his guardian taught him grace in
discourse
that he might talk graciously
converse well
talk agreeably with any he met

with his flute his smoking tube his
flowers he walked the streets
much honored

honored as our lord
treated by all as our lord the great god
entreated with sighs for favors

before him the people bowed and
kissed with reverence the earth

if at any time his body became even a little fat they

gave him brine to drink
so that he became thin
lean and hard and firm

For one year he lived thus
              he went about playing music
              following whatever way he wished
              by day or by night

eight young men were given him as companions
              four shorn as slaves
              four crowned warriors

and Moctezuma himself adorned the young man
              arrayed him as the god
              ornamented him
              in great pomp with costly
              articles in all truth
              arrayed like the beloved god himself

              His face was anointed with black
              ("He fasts with blackened face")
              his cheeks black-smeared
              white feathers upon his head soft
              eagle down attached to his hair
              his long hair that fell to his loins
              and flowers also upon his head a crown
              of flowers flowers like popped corn
              sweet smelling flowers that hung mantling
              both shoulders
              ("the flowery garment")

              and curved ear pendants of gold and shell
              earplugs of turquoise mosaic
              a necklace of shells and a breast ornament of

white sea shells
a lip plug of slender snail shell
golden bracelets on each upper arm and on
        both
wrists bracelets with precious stones
        wide-banded
covering all the forearm

a cape of net fringed with brown cotton
and a costly breechclout reaching to the
calves of his legs and on each leg
golden bells
jingling and ringing whenever he ran and
sandals princely sandals with
ocelot-skin ears

Then
when the feast of the month of Toxcatl
the feast of the great god Tezcatlipoca was
drawing near approaching him
coming toward him

then he was married to four women
chosen women

for twenty days he lived
with these women lying
with them

during this time he began to scatter here
and there
drop and throw aside
the ornaments that adorned him

and at this time his hair

was shorn about his forehead
tufted in a warlock at his forehead and to the long hair
down his back were tied red thongs with single feathers of the
quetzal

    and now five days before the feast of the great Tezcatlipoca
        they began
singing and dancing
the young god and his companions and
his women

on the first day they danced and sang at
Tecanman
on the second day at
Titlacauan
on the third day at Tepetzinco in the midst of
the lagoon
on the fourth at Tepepulco

    Then
    then on the fifth day he embarked
    in a canoe his women beside him
    (to keep him merry)
    he floated to the shore at Caualtepec

and here he was abandoned by his women
from here the women returned

    Now with his companions his pages
    he arrived at the temple of Tlacochcalco
    and by himself
    of his own free will
    ascended its steps

        at the first step he stopped and broke
        his flute

his music stopped

at another step he broke and threw down
his smoking tube

at each step
he broke and scattered the belongings
left to him
until

at the summit of the steps nothing
was left to him nothing

and there
at the summit of the temple steps
the priests fell upon him

they threw him on his back upon
the stone

they cut open his breast tore out
his heart and raised it to the sun
in offering

later his severed head was
impaled upon the skull rack

Thus he ended his life
in the adornment of death so is betokened our life on earth

For whoever rejoices in possessions and
prosperity
sweet things and riches
ends in nothing and in misery

For says the god himself
Tezcatlipoca
"No one takes with him into death
the good things of life"

Adapted from Book II of Fray Bernardino de Sahagun, *General History of the Things of New Spain;* the *Florentine Codex,* translated by Charles E. Dibble and Arthur J. O. Anderson, Santa Fe, 1950 ff.

NAHUATL: *A Song of Nezahualcoyotl*

Listen
I the singer the noble Nezahualcoyotl lament
the brevity of all life the brief time
of my own power

O restless and striving man when your death shall come your
world shall fall into darkness and oblivion

That great man that great conqueror Tezozomoc
(at the age of a hundred years)
his palaces and gardens surely so one thought
would last forever
but now already are dry and ruined
as everything must end in death
as all life is illusion and deception in the end

Sad and impressive indeed to reflect on that great Tezozomoc
he grew like a willow tree rising so high above the grass the
flowers of spring
rejoicing for so long in life and mighty power
until at last the storm wind of death tore him even
him from his roots
dashed him in fragments to the ground
now for all time he is vanished withered
and decayed

In these lamentations in this sad song
I call to mind that which takes place in the spring compare
the life of spring with the fall and death of great Tezozomoc
none seeing this can refrain from tears and weeping
that these flowers these rich colors this rich life
are only bouquets that pass from hand to hand that

wither even in our own short lifetime

You sons of strong people ponder this think
upon this
this that takes place in spring and the
death and oblivion which overtook great Tezozomoc

none can refrain from tears and weeping that these flowers
these rich delights are only bouquets that pass from hand to hand
dying even in our own short lifetime

Let the birds enjoy with their melodies this house
of flowery spring let the butterflies drink
the nectar of its flowers

Adapted from Daniel G. Brinton, *Ancient Nahuatl Poetry,* Philadelphia, 1887. This song, attributed to the famous Nezahualcoyotl, was supposed to have been sung on the occasion of a feast when the foundations were laid for Nezahualcoyotl's famous palace. His is the most celebrated name from the pre-Conquest Valley of Mexico: as poet, hero of legend and romance, "king" of the city of Texcoco, beloved husband of a hundred wives; one of his popular names was Acolmixtli ("Lion Arm"), another was Yoyontzin ("Beautiful Fucker").

NAHUATL: *A Song of Nezahualcoyotl*

the riches of this world are only lent to us

the things that are so good to enjoy we do not own

the sun pours down gold
fountains pour out green water
colors touch us like fingers
of green quetzal wings

none of this can we own for more than a day

none of these beautiful things can we keep for more than an hour

one thing alone we can own forever
the memory of the just
the remembrance of a good act
the good remembrance of a just man

this one thing alone will never be taken away from us

will never die

Credited to the famous Nezahualcoyotl, d. 1472, "king" of Texcoco in the Valley of Mexico, adapted here from a version translated by Fanny Calderon for William H. Prescott and printed by him in a Note to his *Conquest of Mexico*.

MAYA: *Bitter Chant*

           eat eat   while there is bread
           drink drink   while there is water
a day comes when dust will darken the air
                       when
              a blight will wither the land
                            a cloud arise
                            a mountain lifted
                            by a strong man
                            ruin fall upon all
                  when
        the tender leaf will be destroyed
                            eyes closed in death

when we shall see three signs hanging on a tree
father
       son
          grandson
               hanging dead on the same tree
when war will appear
and the people be scattered abroad in the forest

From a translation in Daniel G. Brinton, *Essays of an Americanist,* Philadelphia, 1890.

MAYA: *A Sad Song*

then began the building of the church
here in the center of Tihoo
great labor is the destiny of the katun

then began the execution by hanging
and the fire at the ends of their hands

then also came ropes and cords into the world

then came the children of the younger brothers
under the hardship of legal summons and tribute

tribute was introduced on a large scale

and Christianity was introduced on a large scale

then the seven sacraments of god's word were established

RECEIVE YOUR GUESTS HEARTILY
OUR ELDER BROTHERS COME!

From a translation in Ralph L. Roys, *The Book of Chilam Balam of Chumayel,* Washington, D.C., 1933, in comparison with a revision by Herbert J. Spinden. These lines are from the "Prophecy of Katun 9 Ahau," covering events from 1556 to 1575, when persecution under Spanish conquerors had begun.

NAHUATL: *Song (Fragment)*

What was I born for
why did I leave the house of god
to come to earth?
To be like this
miserable?

Truly I should never have been born
truly I should never have come to earth
is this what I should say?

What shall I do
(you who hear me)
what do you think
(you?)

Should I continue to struggle in this
life on the earth?
Is it my destiny
sadness
my heart suffering?

Oh friend of mine
will you give me help
on this earth?

Freely translated from Angel Maria Garibay K., *Poesia Nahuatl*, Mexico 1964. These are the first three stanzas of poem number 36, originally from a manuscript of Juan Bautista de Pomar, *Romances de los Señores de la Nueva España*, compiled in Texcoco between 1575 and 1580.

NAHUATL: *Fragments, Three Versions*

(Nic chalchiuhcozcameca quenmach totóma in
nocuic)
I unwind my song like a string of jade jewels
or
I unwind my song like a string of precious jewels
or
I see my song unwinding in a thousand directions,
like a string of precious
stones

(Xiuhcóyólizitzilica in teocuitlahuehuetl)
the turquoise bells tinkling in the golden drum
or
the golden drum's turquoise-bell-tinkling
or
the silver drum sounds like bells of turquoise

(Ayauhcocamalotonameyotimani)
mist rainbow shining there is
or
the brightness of the rainbow is there
or
it glows like the rainbow

(Tlauhquéchollaztalehualto tonatoc)
ochre-red bird a heron reverently rising up in flight
or
it (or he) shone like a noble red-winged heron in flight
or
it is gleaming red like the tlahquechol bird

From Brinton, *Ancient Nahuatl Poetry,* Philadelphia, 1887. The first two versions of each line are variant versions by Brinton, and the third version of each line is a translation by Father Horatio Carochi from his *Grammar of the Nahuatl Language,* published in 1645. The original Nahuatl lines, as can be seen, are here all made up of long compound words.

NAHUATL: *Hymn for Fasting*

The flower in my heart blossoms in the middle of the night

The goddess has satisfied her passion the carnal goddess is content

I was born in Paradise I come from the land of flowers

I am a new and only flower

I was born from water I came born as a mortal as a youth as a
new god

I shone forth as the sun my mother dwelt in the house of the dawn
a new flower

I came forth on the earth in the marketplace as a mortal even I

Rest beneath flowers bright as the quetzal bird

Listen to the quechol singing to the gods singing by the river

Hear its flute along the river in the river's house of reeds

Our flesh is a flower a flower in a place of flowers

It cannot be that flowers cease from dying

He plays the ball game the servant of marvelous skill he plays at
ball

Youths make yourselves equal in the ball court to your forebears

They carry the bird of flowers to the market she startles my heart

Where the merchants sell green jade earrings she is to be seen

Sleep sleep sleep I fold my hands to sleep

I O woman sleep

Adapted from Daniel G. Brinton, *Rig Veda Americanus,* Philadelphia, 1890.

DOMINICA CARIB: *A Dance*

. . . the agaya crab will crawl up a girl's leg
and make her pregnant for him

oh it likes women
the agaya

> so sing
> touk-teka-touk
> cric-crac
> tim-tim

and make . . .

> touk-teka-touk
> cric-crac
> tim-tim

and make . . .

> touk-teka-touk
> cric-crac
> tim-tim

and makes the spirits dance. . . .

Adapted from Douglas Taylor, *The Caribs of Dominica, BAE Bulletin 119,* Washington, D.C., 1938.

DOMINICA CARIB: *A Song*

Sure I sucked the tote totes
            of my maman
            to four years old and after

Sure I buy poudre pine tortue
            that is the powdered member
            of the potent turtle
            when I want to be with my woman

Sure you are disgusted

But I am disgusted I too
            when you people put dirt of your bowels
            and dirt of your beasts' bowels
            on your gardens

            Zombie piai
                zombie piai

            Fearful that is
                fearful

Adapted from Douglas Taylor, *The Caribs of Dominica, BAE Bulletin 119,* Washington, D.C., 1938.

PIMA: *Feast Song*

I stand straight
           singing my shining song
                      to the gods

Harlots come running
           holding blue flowers
                      talking in whispers

                (Singers now appear, in two files,
                men and women apart.)

Along the crooked road I'm going
along the crooked road I'm going
                going to the rainbows
                westward to the rainbows
                swinging my arms

Adapted from the literal translation in Frank Russell, "The Pima Indians," *Twenty-sixth Annual BAE Report,* Washington, D.C., 1908.

PIMA: *A Dancing Song*

Dizzy I run into the bog water
there tadpoles sing among the reeds
tadpoles wearing girdles of bark
                              there singing

In the evening land a very blue dragonfly
hanging on the water top
touching in his tail

There I run in rattling darkness
cactus flowers in my hair
in rattling darkness
                              darkness rattling
running to that singing place

Adapted from the literal translation in Russell, "The Pima Indians."

PIMA: *Medicine Song (Gila Monster Song)*

Pitiable prostitute woman though I am
my soul flowers with evening
whore
my heart flowers

Around those two stones standing there
came a black wind roaring
driving the birds
back and forth fluttering

On the top of that white place there
green frogs are singing
under blue clouds

so many singing

Adapted from the literal translation in Russell, "The
Pima Indians."

PIMA: *Medicine Song (Fragment)*

The yellow wren himself pulled out his feathers
with them he made me a prostitute
a whore running over the land
with feathers on my head
with my hands clasped

Blue Bird drifted at the edge of the land
lying on the blue wind

White Wind ran in wind
blowing dust

Moons are shining in me here
you men will see
      you women will see
the far distant moon come to meet me
when I blow upon this blue reed

> Adapted from the literal translation in Russell, "The
> Pima Indians."

PIMA: *Hunting Song*

The white morning standing
the white morning standing
I arose to go

The blue evening falling
the blue evening falling
I arose to go

Datura leaves, datura leaves
I that eat them dizzy stagger run
Datura flowers, datura flowers
I that drink them drunk stagger run

The great man named Bow-remaining
following here overtook and killed me
here cut and threw my horns away

The great man named Reed-remaining
following here overtook and killed me
here cut and threw my feet away

Fly made crazy, fly made crazy
drop there buzz there
You butterfly made drunk, butterfly drunk
there now drop there
fall there drunk
while you open and shut your wings

Adapted from the literal translation in Russell, "The Pima Indians."

PIMA: *A Feast Song*

        shining morning up there come
        shining morning up there come
                reaching to the pleiades

Sun comes
      rises high
           lifting moon

   bluebird running

many women
        carrying clouds
            upon their heads

        dancing clouds atop their heads

        magic spider ties the sun
                rolls the moon

        gray spider
        stands there
              turns
                goes

See the green cane rising higher.

Adapted from the literal translation in Russell, "The Pima Indians."

PAPAGO: *Elegy Dream Song*

In the great night my heart will go out
darkness will come toward me
      with a sound of rattling
in the great night my heart will go out

I am running toward a range of low mountains
from those mountain tops I will see the dawn

I die and lie dead here

I die and lie dead here!

Adapted from Frances Densmore, *Papago Music, BAE
Bulletin 90*, Washington, D.C., 1929.

HOPI: *Kachina Song*

Yellow butterflies for corn blossoms
                (with flower-painted maidens' faces)
Blue butterflies over bean blossoms
                (with pollen-painted maidens' faces)
Yellow and blue hovering, hovering,

Wild bees singing in and out

Over all black thunder hanging

Over all downpouring rain

Adapted from Natalie Curtis, *The Indians' Book,* New York, 1907, in comparison with a literal translation made with the consultation of Rev. H. R. Voth. The song was composed and sung by a young poet of the time, Koianimptiwa, for a Korosta Kachina Dance, a corn-planting dance in which the kachinas wear rainbow masks.

HOPI: *Tale*

I
A long time ago a beautiful maiden lived in the village of Oraibi
in the northern part of the village

All the young men wanted to marry her but she refused them all

The young men would gather flowers
      some would go even long distances to find rare flowers and
          even
      these they offered to her
      but she refused them all

Far away in the north the Yellow Cloud chief heard of her

He prepared a beautiful bridal outfit
                        (two robes)
                        (moccasins)
                        (a knotted belt and a reed
                              mat)

He brought it to the village and offered it to the maiden
      but she refused

The Blue Cloud chief of the west offered a bridal outfit (blue)
Red Cloud chief of the south offered a bridal outfit (red)
White Cloud chief of the east offered a bridal outfit (white)
Black Cloud chief from above offered a bridal outfit (black)
Gray Cloud chief from below offered a bridal outfit (gray)

She refused them all

Now far away in the south the rain god Pavayoykashi heard of her

He painted himself and dressed like the flute players
    brilliantly
    like the Powamuy dancers
    like certain Kachinas
    he painted a black line over his cheeks and nose
    he took a bow and he took arrows in a quiver of panther skin

He took these things to the maiden

She liked him she accepted these things from him
she liked him she promised to speak to her parents

II
Now at that time Coyote Old Man lived west of the village
(they call that place Coyote Gap today)

Secretly Coyote went to the house of Pavayoykashi
    secretly he stole costume and ornaments

Secretly he dressed and painted like Pavayoykashi
    dressed and painted like Pavayoykashi he went to the
        maiden's house

She was deceived
    she was deceived by Coyote Old Man dressed and painted
        like Pavayoykashi her lover
    willingly she went with him to his house

Pavayoykashi his costume and ornaments stolen looked
    for the tracks of the thief he followed
    the tracks of the thief to the house of the maiden
    and to the house of Coyote

And all the young men of the village joined to kill Old Man
    Coyote

furious that he had stolen the beautiful girl who had refused them
    all

But Coyote escaped he escaped them all
    he escaped and ran to the western mesa to
    the mesa west of the village and safe on the mesa
    he shouted back in derision
    in derision grasping his genitals and showing his genitals
    with which he had enjoyed their beautiful maiden

He escaped and disappeared
he ran away across the mesa

Then Pavayoykashi brought a storm
    a strong storm with wind and rain and thunder
    and he himself hidden in the thunder

Far and wide he rode the storm and when he found Old Man
    Coyote he struck him dead
he struck him dead from the storm
he struck him dead with lightning from the storm

Adapted from H. R. Voth, *The Traditions of the Hopi*,
Field Columbian Museum Publication 96, Anthro-
pological Series, Vol. VIII, Chicago, 1905.

ZUÑI: *Storm Song*

Cover my earth mother
four times with many flowers

Cover the heavens
with high-piled clouds

Cover the earth with fog
cover the earth with rains

Cover the earth with great rains
cover the earth with lightnings

Let thunder drum over all the earth
let thunder be heard

Let thunder drum over all
over all the six directions of the earth

Adapted from Matilda Coxe Stevenson, "The Zuñi
Indians," *Twenty-third Annual BAE Report,* Washing-
ton, D.C., 1904.

SANTO DOMINGO PUEBLO:
Two Fragments of Songs

All the white-cloud eagles
Lift me up with your wings
Take me to the entrance to the earth
All you eagles
Lift me up with your wings
Lift me high over the world
Let no one see where you are taking me
   far to the southwest
    where our fathers and mothers have gone (before me)
Take me there with your wings
Place me there with your wings.

   he begins to move   the man who will do the whipping
   he begins to move and moves   he becomes me myself
   now opening my eyes now a member of the Shaiak
   now with the right and duty to take the place   of a
     spirit
   with my mother
   with my mother the bear

Slightly revised from Frances Densmore, *Music of Santo Domingo Pueblo, New Mexico, Southwest Museum Papers No. 12,* Los Angeles, 1938.

TEWA: *Song of the Sky Loom*

Oh our Mother the Earth oh our Father the Sky
Your children are we
    with tired backs we bring you the gifts you love

So weave for us a garment of brightness

May the warp be the white light of morning
May the weft be the red light of evening
May the fringes be the falling rain
May the border be the standing rainbow

Weave for us this bright garment
that we may walk where birds sing
    where grass is green

Oh our Mother the Earth oh our Father the Sky

Slightly revised from Herbert J. Spinden, *Songs of the Tewa*, New York, 1933.

COCHITI: *Bird and Toad Play Hide and Seek*

Down by the river there lived a little bird

A toad lived near by

    I will ask this bird to play hide and seek with me
    said Toad

He went to the river and there was the little bird
teetering back and forth

    What a pretty way you have of moving your body
    said Toad

    Is it a pretty way
    asked Bird

    Yes
    said Toad
    so shall we play hide and seek

    Yes
    said Bird
    let's play hide and seek

    First I must go back home
    and tell mother
    said Toad

    I must tell my mother so she won't be looking for me
    I must tell her so she won't be thinking somebody has killed
        me

Then hurry
said Bird

So Toad hopped home and said

Mother I came to tell you that down
at the river there is a sandy place
and we are going to play hide and seek
that's what I came to tell you

His mother said
Be sure not to go far

Somebody might kill you

No mother
said Toad

I'll stay right there
in that sandy place

Then Toad went back to Bird and said

Now come on and
we will play

and they went to a sandy place by the river

They were both laughing and having a good time

Now we'll start
said Toad
you be first

No
said Bird
you be first

You invited me

So Toad went to hide

    When you are hidden
    Bird said
    you call to me

So Toad covered himself all up with sand
and when he was ready
he called and said

    All right
    I am ready

Bird came to hunt for him
she came right to where he was
but couldn't find him

    Where is he hiding
    said Bird

She stepped right on Toad
and almost fell over

    Now look
    I have found an arrow head
    to take to my grandfather for a knife

    I am not an arrow head
    said Toad
    I am Toad

Then Bird dug him out
and they both laughed and laughed

    Now it is your turn Bird
    said Toad

So Bird went to the same sandy place
and hid in the same place where Toad had been

She left just her bill sticking out

    Now I am ready Toad
    said Bird

Toad came looking for her
he looked everywhere
he searched and searched
he couldn't find a sign of her

He hopped up and down and back and forth
and he ran his stomach right against Bird's bill

    Now look
    I have found an awl for my grandfather
    to fix his shoes with

He began to pull as hard as he could

    I am not an awl
    said Bird
    I am Bird

They laughed and laughed

So they both found each other
and Toad went home to his mother
safe and well

and Bird stayed at the river
where she lived

Adapted from Ruth Benedict, *Tales of the Cochiti In-
dians, BAE Bulletin 98,* Washington, D.C., 1931.

COCHITI: *Coyote and Beaver Exchange Wives*

Old Coyote and Old Coyote Woman lived
on one side of the hill

Old Beaver and Old Beaver Woman lived on
the other side of the hill

One night it was snowing

I will invite my brother Beaver to go hunting
said Old Coyote

and whoever hunts the best will have the other's wife
said Old Coyote

So he went to see Old Beaver

> We'll go hunting and if we kill rabbits
> we'll bring them to our wives
> said Old Coyote

> I'll take mine to your wife and
> you take yours to my wife

Old Beaver smoked a while

> All right
> said Old Beaver

> You go first, since you invited me

> All right I will go in the morning
> said Old Coyote

> I will go hunting for you

he said to Old Beaver Woman

I will sing a song for you
so you may kill many rabbits
said Old Beaver Woman

So Old Coyote was gone all day hunting

In the evening Old Beaver Woman sang her song
        Old Coyote Old Coyote come and sleep with me
        Old Coyote Old Coyote come make love to me

Then she howled like a coyote
    Woo-wu!wu!wu!woooooo-wook-wike-yike-yiyiyiyi-woooooo-
        woo!

He won't kill anything
said Old Beaver

He isn't any hunter
It won't do you any good to sing

But Beaver woman waited and waited
singing and singing

But Old Coyote killed nothing at all
so he never appeared at all

The next day Old Beaver went hunting

He told Old Coyote Woman to wait for him
He told her he was going to kill rabbits for her

Then he hunted
and killed so many rabbits he could hardly carry them

and hardly able to carry them
he brought them to Coyote's house

Old Coyote Woman, here are the rabbits

Thank you thank you Old Man Beaver

They went straight into the inner
room and left Old Man Coyote by himself

Old Man Coyote was unhappy

They gave him his supper and then
they went in to bed

Old Beaver Man started putting his penis into
Old Coyote Woman and
Old Coyote Woman cried out and cried out at the
top of her voice

Old Beaver don't you hurt my wife
said Old Coyote

    Shut up Old Man Coyote
    said Coyote Woman
    I am crying out because I like it

    You old fool
    said Coyote Woman

When they were finished Old Beaver Man came out and
said to Old Coyote

    We won't have bad feelings
    you know this was your idea

So they all remained friends
the same as ever

Adapted from Ruth Benedict, *Tales of the Cochiti Indians, BAE Bulletin 98*, Washington, D.C., 1931.

TAOS: *The Sacred Lands of the Blue Lake Forest*

The Blue Lake lands, this is our church.
We worship there so our Indian life can exist.
Indian customs, Indian features.
We have no power to convert our complexion.
We like to preserve.
These sacred lands are more to us than any other church.
Churches are man-made, but this is God's.

Statement made to me by Paul Bernal, secretary and interpreter for the Taos Pueblo Council, when I attended a meeting of the council in the spring of 1969.

MESCALERO APACHE: *Dawn Song*
(*from the Gotal Ceremony*)

The black turkey in the east spreads his tail
The tips of his beautiful tail are the white dawn

Boys are sent running to us from the dawn
They wear yellow shoes of sunbeams

They dance on streams of sunbeams

Girls are sent dancing to us from the rainbow
They wear shirts of yellow

They dance above us the dawn maidens

The sides of the mountains turn to green
The tops of the mountains turn to yellow

And now above us on the beautiful mountains it is dawn.

Adapted from P. E. Goddard, "Gotal—A Mescalero
Apache Ceremony," in *Putnam Anniversary Volume,*
New York, 1909.

NAVAJO: *Toad Man's Song*
from the Beauty Way

Down below I am sitting
                (earth, sky, Tortoise)
                (short rainbow, growing things, falling
                    rain)
                (beads swinging, perfect shell disk)
                down below I am sitting

Sky
Mount Taylor
Mountain Lion
            (long rainbow, falling rain, growing things)
            (swinging beads, perfect shell disk)
            (call of Cornbeetle)
            down below I sit

Badger
Yellow-bill
Badger tail
          (lighting struck close by)
          (growing things, falling rain)
          (beads swinging, perfect shell disk)
          down below I am sitting
                rain is close
                rain passed by
                Bear
                Salamander
                swinging beads
                shell disk
                rainbow
                falling rain
                growing things

Adapted from Father Berard Haile and Leland C. Wyman, *Beautyway*, New York, 1957.

NAVAJO: *The War God's Horse Song*

I am the Turquoise Woman's son

On top of Belted Mountain beautiful horses
slim like a weasel

My horse has a hoof like striped agate
his fetlock is like fine eagle plume
his legs are like quick lightning

My horse's body is like an eagle-feathered arrow

My horse has a tail like a trailing black cloud

I put flexible goods on my horse's back

The Holy Wind blows through his mane
his mane is made of rainbows

My horse's ears are made of round corn

My horse's eyes are made of stars

My horse's head is made of mixed waters
    (from the holy waters)
    (he never knows thirst)

My horse's teeth are made of white shell

The long rainbow is in his mouth for a bridle
with it I guide him

When my horse neighs
different-colored horses follow

When my horse neighs
different-colored sheep follow

I am wealthy from my horse

Before me peaceful
Behind me peaceful
Under me peaceful
Over me peaceful
Around me peaceful
Peaceful voice when he neighs
I am everlasting and peaceful
I stand for my horse

Adapted from Dane and Mary Roberts Coolidge, *The Navaho Indians,* Boston, 1930. The words to the song were furnished by Tall Kiaah'ni, and interpreted by Louis Watchman.

NAVAJO: *From the Night Chant*

In beauty
>   you shall be my representation

In beauty
>   you shall be my song

In beauty
>   you shall be my medicine

In beauty
>   my holy medicine

Adapted from Washington Matthews, *The Night Chant, A Navaho Ceremony, Memoirs of the American Museum of Natural History,* Vol. VI, New York, 1902.

NAVAJO: *Concerning Wisdom, A Fragment*

I perform the Beauty Way.
I am over eighty years old.
I have been learning since I was eleven years old.
I want some one to learn what I have been learning.

Statement of Dan Yazzie, a medicine man, quoted in
the Rough Rock Demonstration School's *Rough Rock
News,* Chinle, Arizona, September 24, 1969. The Beauty
Way is a curing chant, a major ceremonial.

NAVAJO: *Lines from the Wind Chant*

The patient was twice bathed, sacredly.

Then his body was painted with the sun on his breast
                and the wind above,
                the moon on his back,
                arrows on his arms,
                snakes on his legs
                and on each shoulder a white cross.

A prayer plume they tied to his head
and they painted his face,
                white on the forehead,
                red across the eyes,
                yellow across the chin.

They mixed herbs
                and the Blue Jay came
                and the Whirling Winds.

The singer stroked the patient's body
and pressed his body to the patient's body.

Have you learned? they asked him
and he answered, Yes.

They sang all night, and the patient learned
and was well.

Then he was told to be sure and remember all that he had been
      taught,
for everything forgotten went back to the gods.

KIOWA: *A Peyote Thought*

The Peyote Man prays
to an unknown mystery
he has no name for it
        but life

The Peyote Man prays
to a great light
to the great light
to understand the light
        within himself

Adapted from Willard Rhodes, *Music of the American Indian: Kiowa,* Library of Congress, Archives of American Folksong, c. 1955, quoting the description of a "peyote painting" by Monroe Tsa Toke, the artist, d. 1937. Peyote was introduced into the United States by the Kiowas as an element in a new religious cult to take the place of the sun dance, banned in the 1880's and 90's.

KIOWA: *A Peyote Vision*

In the morning at dawn
when the Water Bird fan is used
when the Water Song is sung
the priest's face disappears

in its place is the Water Bird

     singing

perched upon a staff
the peyote gourd beneath

Adapted from Willard Rhodes, *Kiowa Music,* quoting Monroe Tsa Toke.

PAWNEE: *The Birth of Dawn, from the* Hako

Earth our mother, breathe forth life
        all night sleeping
        now awaking
        in the east
        now see the dawn

Earth our mother, breathe and waken
        leaves are stirring
        all things moving
        new day coming
        life renewing

Eagle soaring, see the morning
        see the new mysterious morning
        something marvelous and sacred
        though it happens every day
        Dawn the child of God and Darkness

Adapted from Alice C. Fletcher, "The Hako, a Paw-
nee Ceremony," *Twenty-second Annual BAE Report,*
Washington, D.C., 1904.

FROM THE HAKO (PAWNEE, OSAGE, OMAHA): *Invoking the Powers*

Remember, remember the circle of the sky
        the stars and the brown eagle
        the supernatural winds
        breathing night and day
        from the four directions

Remember, remember the great life of the sun
        breathing on the earth
        it lies upon the earth
        to bring out life upon the earth
        life covering the earth

Remember, remember the sacredness of things
        running streams and dwellings
        the young within the nest
        a hearth for sacred fire
        the holy flame of fire

> Adapted from Fletcher, *Twenty-second Annual BAE Report.*

PAWNEE: *Recitation of War Honors*

(The chief himself was the first to take up the medicine bundle and tied it around his waist. He now took up his bow and arrows; then he squatted down upon the ground; then he began to grunt, his head and shoulders shaking to keep time with the drumming. Finally, he arose and danced. When the singing ceased, the chief spoke in a loud voice.)

I speak of a certain place
    I killed an eagle
    I consecrated the eagle
    that same year I killed an enemy
    and took his scalp
    and consecrated the scalp to the gods in the heavens
    and the gods received my smoke

I speak of a certain place
    I killed a wildcat
    and consecrated it
    and that same year I went upon the warpath
    and captured ponies
    when I returned to the village
    I took one pony and gave it to the priest

I speak of a certain place
    I killed a raccoon
    I consecrated it to the gods in the heavens
    that same year I went on the warpath
    and captured many ponies
    upon my return to the village
    I gave four horses to different men

The gods in the heavens have heard me

They will make the path straight for you to do likewise.

Adapted from James R. Murie, *Pawnie Indian So-
cieties, Anthropological Papers, American Museum of
Natural History,* Vol. XI, New York, 1914.

P A W N E E : *Buffalo Dance Song*

Listen
the song of the aged father

The song
of the aged beloved

Our father
the buffalo heavy with age

Heavy with age
endlessly walking

Too heavy
to rise again if he should fall

Walking forever
walking forever

Humped high with age
head bent with age

Heavy with age
heavy with age

Aged buffalo
my aged father

Adapted from a translation by Densmore in *Pawnee
Music, BAE Bulletin 93,* Washington, D.C., 1929.

OSAGE: *Buffalo Myth*

O grandfather come to us
come down to us
O grandfather give us a suitable
symbol for peace

and the red god had with him his red plume
the red of dawn and peace
which he swiftly took from its sacred cover
and shot it into the mouth of the angry bull
where it lodged
by the left of his tongue
lengthwise
by the left of his tongue

and then no longer
the buffalo
pawed the earth in anger

no longer thunder rolled
from the ridge pole overhead

no longer
grandfather the buffalo
threw dust with his foot in anger

but he lowered his tail
the buffalo

which he had lifted in anger

and stood subdued by the magic of peace

Freely adapted from a translation by Francis La
Flesche, in "The Osage Tribe: Rite of the Chiefs:
Sayings of the Ancient Men," *Thirty-sixth Annual
BAE Report,* Washington, D.C., 1921. These lines are
from the song of the Buffalo Bull gens, "Tho-xe Pa
Thi-hon."

OSAGE: *From a Legend*

Then up sprang the blazing star from the earth
up to the sky where it stood in all its beauty
pleasing to look upon

From Francis La Flesche, "The Osage Tribe: Two
Versions of the Child-Naming Rite" in *Forty-third
BAE Report*, Washington, D.C., 1928.

O S A G E : *Fragment from the Child-naming Rites*

The Chief Messenger
hastened to the side of the heavens where lay the Dog Star
      (as though suspended in the sky)
and returned with him to the people

The people called to him saying
Grandfather Grandfather
the little ones have nothing of which to make their bodies

Then at that very time the Dog Star replied
      The little ones shall make of me their bodies

      See my toes that are gathered closely together
      I have not folded them together without a purpose

      When the little ones make of me their bodies
      when they become aged
      then in their toes closely folded together
      they shall see the sign of old age. . . .

      And in their ankles and thighs and
      shoulders (drawn close together)
      and the corners of their mouth
      and the folds in the corners of their eyes
      the tip of their nose and the hair on the crown of the
            head
      in all their body from the beginning
      they shall see the sign of old age. . . .

There comes then a time
when a calm and peaceful day descends upon me

so shall there come to these little ones
a calm and peaceful day

Adapted from Francis La Flesche, "The Osage Tribe:
Two Versions of the Child-Naming Rite," *Forty-third
BAE Report*, Washington, D.C., 1928.

OSAGE: *Processional from the War Ceremony*

Around the earth I go
bearing my mystic emblems

      my mystic pipe I carry
      my pipe (consecrated) to our prayers

      my mystic knife I carry
      (to strike to strike)
      my knife (consecrated) for power

      my mystic club I carry
      (to strike to strike)
      my war club (made of magic)

      my mystic clays
      our four clays (containing) the power of the earth

      bearing my mystic standards
      (our two magic standards)
      the prongs of the great elk
      the great elk of the beginning

      bearing my mystic moccasins
      (the four tufts of grass)

         that will clear our path of war
         clear our path for life

Adapted from Francis La Flesche, *War Ceremony and Peace Ceremony of the Osage Indians, BAE Bulletin 101,* Washington, D.C., 1939.

OMAHA: *Buffalo Song*

In this way came the buffalo tracks
the buffalo tracks that we see
that everywhere we see

the tracks of those feet were made by life
in this way
life that came
in this way

Life to the unborn
first in the belly of the mother
life to the unborn nose
to the unborn face, to the unborn eyes,
life to the unborn horns
life to the living being

Now the little calf is born
filled with life and motion
born filled with life and motion
born the newborn yellow calf
standing on its feet and walks

leaving tracks
leaving footprints
buffalo buffalo
leaving tracks

Adapted from a translation by Francis La Flesche in
"The Omaha Tribe," by Alice C. Fletcher and Francis
La Flesche, *Twenty-seventh Annual BAE Report*,
Washington, D.C., 1911. Portions of this poem were
quoted in my short story "The Buffalo Singer" in *The
North American Review*, Summer, 1964.

OMAHA: *Myth*

Toward the coming of the sun
There the people of every kind gathered,
And great animals of every kind.
Truly all gathered together, all,
Even insects of every description,
Truly all gathered there together,
By what means or manner we know not.

Truly, one alone of all these was the greatest,
Inspiring to all minds,
The great white rock,
Standing and reaching as high as the heavens, wrapped in mist,
Truly as high as the heavens.

Thus my little ones shall speak of me,
As long as they shall travel in life's path,
Thus may they speak of me.
Such were the words, it has been said.

Then next in rank
Thou, male of the crane, stood with thy long beak
And thy neck, none so long,
There with thy beak did thou strike the earth.

This shall be the legend
Of the people of the beginning, the red people,
Thus my little ones shall speak of me.

Then next in rank stood the male gray wolf, whose cry,
Though uttered without effort, truly made the earth tremble,
Even the solid earth to tremble.

Such shall be the legend of the people.

Then next in rank stood Hega, the buzzard, with his red neck.
Calmly he stood, his great wings spread,
Letting the heat of the sun straighten his feathers.

Slowly he flapped his wings,
Then floated away, as though without effort,
Thus displaying a power
(a gift of the great God)
Often to be spoken of by the old men teaching.

Slightly altered from the opening lines of the ritual of
the Omaha Pebble Society, in "The Omaha Tribe," by
Alice C. Fletcher and Francis La Flesche, *Twenty-
seventh Annual BAE Report,* Washington, D.C., 1911.
This ritualistic fragment, say the authors, ". . . bears
the marks of antiquity."

OMAHA: *The Rock (Fragment of a Ritual)*

unmoved
from time without
end
you rest
there in the midst of the paths
in the midst of the winds
you rest
covered with the droppings of birds
grass growing from your feet
your head decked with the down of birds
you rest
in the midst of the winds
you wait
Aged one

Adapted from Alice C. Fletcher and Francis La Flesche, "The Omaha Tribe," in *Twenty-seventh Annual BAE Report,* Washington, D.C., 1911.

MANDAN: *The Man Who Married the Birds*

A man went westward journeying
and he came to a lake
in which were birds

> I will make a trap
> and catch them
> these birds

> First I had better make a house
> and then make the trap

So he went into the woods
to make the house
and there met a porcupine woman
and married her

> I have found lots of birds
> woman
> that we can trap and eat

> > When his house was finished
> > he went to the lake and trapped a bird
> > a goose
> > but instead of killing the goose
> > he married her

> > The next day he went to the lake
> > and in his trap was this time
> > a white goose
> > and he married her also

> > The next day he went to his trap
> > and found a crane
> > and he married her too

The next day he went to the lake again
and there was another bird
a heron
and he married her too

The next day he caught a duck
and married her

and the next day he caught in his trap
another duck
a diving duck with a white bill
and he married her also

So his wife said
the porcupine woman said

How is this?
Where are the birds
for us to eat?
You marry them
you marry them all

The next day the man went to the lake
and caught a little tiny bird
a yellow bird
whom he married

The next day he went and caught
a big bird
whom he married

The man said to his bird wives

We will all dance

The wives said

How shall we dance?
How do you want us to dance?

Wait for me
wait and see

This was in the autumn of the year
The man went and got his arms full
of plumed fox grass
and gave each of his bird wives
as much as she could hold
and white and yellow corn

        Now I have to make a drum
        before we can dance

He went out and saw a leaf
He said

        This will be a drum
        and the cover will be antelope hide
        and around the side a pattern
        a pattern of goose tracks

And like turning over a hand
the leaf turned into a drum
covered with antelope hide
and around the edge
a pattern of goose tracks

Then he took another leaf
and said

        This will be my rattle

And like lifting a finger
the leaf turned into a rattle

Then they all started to dance

The man said to the porcupine woman

his wife the porcupine woman

    You must dance last
    you dance the last one
    you dance behind the birds

        The first goose he had married
        was the leader

    We are going to dance four days
    the dance will be called the Goose Dance
    the Goose Dance

They went out to dance
they danced four times

The second day they went out to dance
and the man sang
he sang every day while they danced
he sang with his eyes closed

        The first goose wife said to him

    Winter is coming
    maybe you mean to kill us

It was late in the year
and while they danced
snow was falling
snowing over the Goose Dance

On the third day the man shut his eyes once more
to sing while they danced

        The first goose wife said

    If you sing
    and shut your eyes again

maybe we should fly away
and save our lives

They went out to dance on the fourth day
and the man shut his eyes again
and sang again

Until that day the birds had always sung with him
but now
but now
they were silent

> They are silent
> my birds
> my bird wives

> They are not singing
> my birds
> my bird wives

> They are silent
> dancing in the snow

So the man opened his eyes
and saw the birds all flying away

He ran after them
calling

> Do not fly away
> my birds
> do not fly away
> I have always loved you

> > but the goose wife
> > and the other goose wife
> > and all the bird wives
> > kept flying away
> > flying away

toward the south

Afterward the man went back to his house
to find the porcupine woman
his wife the porcupine woman

but she was gone too.

Adapted from a tale told by Wolf Head in Frances
Densmore, *Mandan and Hidatsa Music, BAE Bulletin
80,* Washington, D.C., 1923.

MANDAN: *A Bedtime Song for Children*

      that track, look
      that track, look
      whose track is it like
      that track?

      you know whose it is?
      you know whose it is?
      why, old Grandfather Two-teeth
      that's whose it is

(Grandfather Two-teeth he is a beaver)

(if it is then go on and follow it)

      go on and follow and come to a lodge
      and pound on the lodge with worn-out feet
      and with that wriggled bag

what's in the lodge?
      who's in the lodge?
           those tracks, look!

      don't be afraid
      (pound pound pound)

      up high there on the roof of the lodge
      look up there on the roof of the lodge

      don't be afraid
      (pound pound pound!)

      look up there lying up there

big fat small child buffalo calf
with a soft belly-button

don't be afraid now
(POUND POUND POUND)

someone coming someone walking
crumbling sticks
crab shells dancing

we'll knock his eye out
(POUND POUND POUND)

After a literal translation in Densmore, *Mandan and Hidatsa Music, BAE Bulletin 80,* Washington, D.C., 1923.

CHEYENNE: *The Death Song of White Antelope*

Nothing lives long
Nothing lives long
Nothing lives long
Except the earth and the mountains

Adapted from *The Fighting Cheyennes,* by George Bird Grinnell, New York, 1915. White Antelope was a noted war captain of the Cheyennes for almost fifty years. He was killed at the Sand Creek Massacre of 1864 as he stood with folded arms singing this song; his scrotum was made into a tobacco pouch by one of the Colorado Volunteers.

DAKOTA: *Song*

I considered myself a wolf
    but the owls are hooting
        and now
            I fear the night

Adapted from Frances Densmore, *Teton Sioux Music,*
BAE Bulletin 61, Washington, D.C., 1918.

NORTHERN ARAPAHO: *The God-Wagon, A Song from the Flat Pipe Ceremony*

The sacred flat pipe
is the wagon of God
the motion of God
the passing by of God

        looking upon it one's shadow is trans-
               ported
        one's shadow is transported to
        the tranquility of home
        looking upon it one's shadow is at home

  It rests upon four stalks
the sacred flat pipe
        as when
        glowing
        it appeared
        upon the dark waters
        upon the dark waters at the birth of the
               world

  Glowing with beauty
afloat on the waters
        glowing
        in the tranquility of home

    It gave to the people
        its pity
    it called the turtle to heap up land
        for the earth people
        the earth people the Arapaho
    it gave the land to the earth people
        the earth people the Arapaho

It gave them the tranquil land of home

> Wherever it rests on its four-legged altar
> it is at home with the shadows
> it is at home in the tranquil shadows
> with the devout people
> the devout people the Arapaho

Adapted from John G. Carter, *The Northern Arapaho Flat Pipe and the Ceremony of Covering the Pipe, BAE Bulletin 119*, Washington, D.C., 1938.

Three Fragments (QUECHUAN, DAKOTA, OJIBWA)

QUECHUAN: The water bug is drawing
                    the shadows of the evening
                            toward him on the water

DAKOTA: You cannot harm me
                    you cannot harm
                            one who has dreamed a dream like
                            mine

OJIBWA: The bush is sitting under a tree and
                    singing

From *Frances Densmore and American Indian Music,*
Museum of the American Indian, Heye Foundation,
New York, 1968.

OJIBWA: *Firefly Song*

Flickering firefly
          give me light
          light
once more before I sleep

Dancing firefly
          wandering firefly
          light
once more before I sleep

White light sailing
          white light winking
just once more before I sleep

Adapted from Henry R. Schoolcraft, *Historical and Statistical Information, Respecting the History, Condition, and Prospects of the Indian Tribes of the United States,* Philadelphia, 1851-57.

OJIBWA: *Spring Song*

as my eyes
        look over the prairie
                I feel the summer in the spring

From a translation in Frances Densmore, *Chippewa Music—II, BAE Bulletin 53*, Washington, D.C., 1913.

OJIBWA: *Love-charm Song*

1.
I can charm that man
I can cause him to become fascinated

2.
What are you saying to me?
I am dressed in colors of the roses?
and as beautiful as the roses?

3.
I can make him bashful
I do wonder what can be the matter with him
that he is bashful?

4.
I can do this where he may be
under the earth
or in the very center of the earth!

Adapted from Densmore, *Chippewa Music.*

DELAWARE: *From the Walum Olum*

in the beginning of the world
    all men had knowledge cheerfully
    all had leisure
    all thoughts were pleasant

at that time all creatures were friends

        wide waters rushing
        wide to the hills
        everywhere spreading
        waters devouring
        men and all creatures on the flood of the waters

        when the daughter of a spirit came to help
        all then joined together
        all saying
            Come help

in other years all traveled
over the waters of the hard stony sea

all were peaceful long ago

    large and long was the east land
    rich and good

shall we be free and happy then
at the new land?

we want rest and peace and wisdom

Adapted from E. G. Squier, ". . . translation of the
Walum-Olum, or Bark Record of the Lenni Lenape,"
first printed in *The American Whig Review,* New
York, February, 1849; in comparison with Daniel G.
Brinton, *The Lenape and their Legends,* Philadelphia,
1885, Canto I, line 20.

IROQUOIS: *The Tree of the Great Peace*

1. THE TREE (C. 1450)
I am Dekanawideh and with the chiefs of the Five Nations
I plant the Tree of the Great Peace. . . .

Roots have spread out from the Tree of the Great Peace. . . .
the Great White Roots of Peace. . . .

Any man of any nation
may trace the roots to their source and be welcome
to shelter
beneath the Great Peace. . . .

I
Dekanawideh
and the chiefs of our Five Nations of the Great Peace
we now uproot the tallest pine

> into the cavity thereby made
> we cast all weapons of war

> Into the depths of the earth
> into the deep underneath. . . .

> we cast all weapons of war

We bury them from sight forever. . . .
and we plant again the tree. . . .

Thus shall the Great Peace be established. . . .

Adapted from William N. Fenton, ed., *Parker on the Iroquois,* Syracuse, 1968.

II. DEGANAWIDAH'S LAST MESSAGE (C. 1450)

We bind ourselves together
(said Deganawidah)
by taking hold of each other's hands. . . .

Our strength shall be in union
our way the way of reason
righteousness and peace. . . .

Hearken, O chiefs, that peace may continue unto future days. . . .

Have courage. . . .

Think not so much of present advantage
as the future welfare of the people. . . .

When you administer the Law
your skins must be seven thumbs thick
so the envious darts of your enemies may
not penetrate. . . .

Be of strong mind
O chiefs
carry no anger. . . .

Think not forever of yourselves nor of your own generation. . . .

Think of those yet unborn whose faces are coming
from beneath the ground. . . .

Adapted from Paul A. W. Wallace, *The White Roots of Peace*, Philadelphia, 1946.

III. THE DANCING SPEECH OF O-NÓ-SA
(c. 1850)

Many winters ago our wise ancestors predicted that a great
monster
with white eyes
would come from the east and consume the land

They advised their children to plant a tree
with four roots
to the north
to the south
to the east and to the west

and collecting under its shade
to dwell together in unity
and harmony

> Slightly revised from Lewis Henry Morgan, *League of
> the Ho-de-no-sau-nee, or Iroquois,* Rochester, N.Y.,
> 1851.

SENECA: *From the Introduction to the Code of Handsome Lake*

The beginning was early in the moon (of May)
in the year 1800

    It commences now:

        [a man becomes sick]

    The sunlight comes in and he sees it and he thinks "The Creator made this sunshine"

    Now when he thinks of the sunshine and of the Creator he feels a new hope within him

    So now he makes a prayer that he may be able to endure the night

    Now he lives through the night and sees another day

    So then he makes an invocation and prays that he may see the night and it is so

Now the sick man's bed is beside the fire
At night he looks up through the chimney hole and sees the stars
For everything he sees he is thankful

Now at this time the daughter of the sick man and her husband are sitting outside the house

the sick man is within alone

Now the daughter and her husband are cleaning beans for the
        planting

Suddenly they hear from within they hear the sick man exclaim
    "So be it!"

Then they hear him rising in his bed

They think how he is but yellow skin and dried bones

Now they hear him walking over the floor toward the door

Then the daughter looks up and sees her father

He totters
he falls dying

Now they lift him up and carry him back within the house

they dress him for burial

Now he is dead

       [but the next day at noon the dead man returns to life]

   "I believe myself well"
   these are the first words Handsome Lake spoke

Now then he speaks saying

   "Never have I seen such wondrous visions

   Now at first I heard someone speaking
   Some one spoke and said
      'Come out a while'
   and said this three times

   So I called out boldly
      'So be it'
   and rose and went out and there standing in the clear swept
   space I saw three men

   Their cheeks were painted red

   Only a few feathers were in their bonnets

All three were alike and all seemed middle-aged
Never before have I seen such handsome commanding men
they had in one hand bows and arrows as canes

Now in their other hands were huckleberry bushes
and the berries were of every color

    [the beings give him huckleberries of every color to eat
           for strength]

    [they tell him to go to the council house to speak to the
           people there
    the people there will have gathered the early
           strawberries
    they will make a strawberry feast and thank the Creator
           for his recovery]

    "Now the messengers tell me how things
    ought to be upon the earth"

From Fenton, ed., *Parker on the Iroquois*, Syracuse, 1968. This Introduction is followed by the 130 chapters of The Great Message, relating the sixteen years' ministry of the prophet Ganio'daiío (Handsome Lake), and expounding his visions and his precepts for right living. The Handsome Lake religion is still very healthy among certain groups of Iroquois people in and about New York State, particularly the Onondaga, and the Seneca at Tonawanda. Anthony F. C. Wallace, *The Death and Rebirth of the Seneca*, New York, 1970, contains the most recent retelling of the Handsome Lake story.

SENECA: *A Vision of Handsome Lake*

The day was bright when I went into the planted field
Alone I wandered in the planted field

It was the time of the second hoeing

A maiden appeared and clasped me about the neck
saying
     When you leave this earth for the new world above
     we want to follow you

I looked for the maiden
but saw only the long leaves of corn
twined round my shoulders

I understood it was the spirit of the corn
speaking
she the sustainer of life

I replied O spirit
     follow me not

     but remain here upon the earth
     be strong and faithful to your purpose

     Endure

     Do not fail the children of women

It is not time for you to follow

The word I teach is only in its beginning

Slightly altered from Arthur C. Parker, *The Code of Handsome Lake, the Seneca Prophet,* Albany, 1913. Handsome Lake taught a new religion, and brought a literal salvation to the Seneca; he died at Onondaga, New York, in 1815, a few days after relating this, his last vision.

MALECITE: *Tale*

there was once a woman who admired a dog
the dog was handsome
she liked his face

that night the dog turned into a man
he became her husband

never tell anyone I used to be a dog
never mention it at all
he said to his wife

for a long time they lived together
she never thought of him as a dog
she never spoke of it

but one day she saw some dogs in the village
they were all chasing a bitch
everywhere here and there

so she asked her husband if he would like to be one of them
and instantly he said yes and turned back into a dog
and away he ran with the others

Adapted from Frank G. Speck, "Malecite Tales" in
Journal of American Folk-Lore, Vol. 30, No. 108, 1917.

CHEROKEE: *A Spell to Destroy Life*

Listen!

    Now I have come to step over your soul
        (I know your clan)
        (I know your name)
        (I have stolen your spit and buried it under earth)

    I bury your soul under earth

    I cover you over with black rock

    I cover you over with black cloth

    I cover you over with black slabs

    You disappear forever

    Your path leads to the
                Black Coffin
                in the hills of the Darkening Land

So let it be for you

    The clay of the hills covers you
    The black clay of the Darkening Land

    Your soul fades away

    It becomes blue (color of despair)

    When darkness comes your spirit shrivels and dwindles
                  to disappear forever

Listen!

From James Mooney, "The Sacred Formulas of the Cherokees" in *7th Annual BAE Report,* Washington, D.C., 1891. This dread incantation was one of the formulas in the MS notebook, written in Cherokee, bought by Mooney in 1887 from the renowned medicine man, Swimmer (A'yunini).

CHEROKEE: *Love Charm*

Ku!
Listen! you great earth-woman
         great spirit-woman of the white direction (south)
         no one when with you is ever lonely
         you are most beautiful
         your spirit presence has instantly made me white (color
                 of happiness)
         now I am one with whom no one can ever be lonely
         now you have made the path I travel white (color of
                 happiness)
         never can it be lonely
         it shall never become blue (color of sadness)
         you have brought down to me from above this white road
         you have placed me upon it (so that)
         no one shall ever be lonely with me (so that)
         I am wonderfully handsome
         you have put me into a house of whiteness
         it shall always envelop me and
         no one with me shall ever be lonely
         in truth I shall never become blue
         you have instantly caused this to be so with me

         and now there (on the earth) you have made the
                 woman blue
         you have made her path blue for her
         you have veiled her in loneliness
         you bring her down to the earth you
         place her standing upon the earth in her blue road
         wherever she may go you will let loneliness
         cover her you will let her be marked out for
         loneliness where she stands

Ha!   the clan to which I belong is the one alone
allotted for you
woman
with me no one is ever lonely
I am handsome
put your soul into the very center of my soul
woman
never to turn away
(grant that in the midst of men she shall never think of
        them)
my clan is the one clan alone allotted for you
woman
when the seven clans were established

with other men it is (for you) lonely
they are loathsome fit only
for the common polecat
refuse
fit company only for the common oppossum
loathsome
fit company only for the crow
loathsome
fit only to be with the miserable rain-crow (the gloomy
        cuckoo)

all the seven clans make you feel lonely
they are not good looking
they are clothed with refuse
they go about covered with dung
but I I am a man of whiteness
I stand with my face toward the Sun Land
with me no one is ever lonely
I am very handsome
certainly I shall never become blue
the house of whiteness envelops me wherever I go
with me no one is ever lonely

your soul has come into the center of my soul
never to go away
I (and now I tell you my name)
I take your soul

Sge!

Adapted from James Mooney, "The Sacred Formulas of the Cherokees," in *Seventh Annual BAE Report,* Washington, D.C., 1891. This formula is one of some fifty pages of love charms among the manuscripts— written in Cherokee—of the famous medicine man Gatigwanasti, purchased by James Mooney from his son on the Cherokee reservation in North Carolina in 1888.

CREEK: *From a Notarized Deposition Made by Itshas Harjo*

Q. How old are you?

A. I have passed through many days and traveled a long way,
the shadows have fallen all about me and I
can see but dimly.
But my mind is clear and my memory has not failed me.
I cannot count the years I have lived.
All that I know about my age is that I was old enough to
        draw the bow
and kill squirrels at the time of the second emigration of the
Creeks and Cherokees from the old country under
the leadership of Chief Cooweescoowee.
I was born near Eufaula, Alabama, and left there
when about fifteen years of age and the trip
took about a year,
for the peaches were green when we left Alabama
and the wild onions plentiful here when we arrived.

> Slightly adapted from a deposition dictated to Alexan-
> der Posey, notary public and official interpreter, and
> published in Alexander Lawrence Posey, *Poems,*
> Topeka, Kansas, 1910.

NATCHEZ: *The Cannibal's Seven Sons*

A cannibal an ogre had seven sons
who one time stole some of his beaver meat
so the terrible man the father
took them to a high cliff above a creek
and threw them down
six died but one escaped.

The son who escaped went along at night
and climbed a tree to stay in it at night
but in the morning he saw he had climbed
not a tree but the horn of a snake.

He was afraid to climb down, with the snake below.

People came by in canoes
some people with crooked legs
some with crooked hips
singing songs about these crooked bones.

Some were all blind in one eye
these people looked up at him and said
He has no sense
to sit up on the horns of a snake.

A canoe-load of young women came along
and drifted close to him
and told him to spit to them
which he did and his spit hit only the edge of the canoe
so they drifted nearer.

They said to spit again
and he spit into the middle of the canoe

so they told him to jump in
and he jumped in
and landed right in the middle of the canoe.

He married one of these girls
they had a child
while they were still going along.

Along the river lived the mother of this boy
she had been tormented
by animals such as rats
coming to her and calling out
that they were her children who had been drowned.

Now she only cried and refused to look at anyone
not wanting to be fooled again
but her son
with his wife and her child in her arms
came to the place and landed.

The son said to his mother
mother I have come back
but she said crying
that is what you always say you red rats.

But the son persisted
until at last the mother looked around
and she saw them.

Then she took her grandchild in her arms and danced
and afterward they all went on in the canoe.

Down the river at the house of a chief
the chief called to them
he told them to come up.

They went up
only after the chief made his wives all lie down side by side
so they could walk on them when they went up.

This was done and the travelers
walked up to the chief's house
treading so heavily upon the women lying there
that the women lying there all farted
as the travelers walked up step by step.

The chief wanted to marry the mother too
and he did so.

But he had taken out the eyes of his other wives
and he wanted to take out her eyes too
which the son would not allow
so the chief sent the son some place else.

When the son came back
he found the chief had had his mother's eyeballs taken out
so he hunted around and found them
and put them back in.

Then the chief ordered the son to be taken another place
and again removed the mother's eyes.

And the son came back and found his mother
his mother again without her eyes
his mother dancing around in front of the chief
who was seated beating on a drum.

So again the son hunted for the eyeballs
and again he found them and replaced them
and then he went to the chief
and took the chief's drum away.

Then he went with his mother to their canoe.

The chief told his other wives to catch them
but having no eyes they ran about
unable to find them at all.

So the fugitives got to their canoe
and started off westward
the son beating on the chief's drum
as they went.

Adapted from John R. Swanton, *Myths and Tales of the Southeastern Indians, BAE Bulletin 88,* Washington, D.C., 1929.

NATCHEZ: *The Tale of the Jealous Brother*

There were two brothers
one had a young wife
he was jealous

One day a big fish ate him
the brother who was jealous
ate him up except for his head

His head kept on singing though
and said to his brother
> Tell my wife
> we can never go together again
> never go together again

> but I will come home in the morning
> singing

The brother went home
and in the morning the head came
flying through the air
singing

> I will kill you
> the head sang
> I will kill you both

So the brother and the young wife
ran away
ran away

They went to the house of a bird
a dirt-dauber
a bird that was a magician

To hide them the dirt-dauber worked
magic
he said to the young wife
    I will turn you into a man

    Fall on the earth
    said the dirt-dauber
    and the wife fell on the earth
    when you rise up you are a man
    said the dirt-dauber
    and the young wife became a man

The head was jealous and jealous
he flew to the dirt-dauber's house

The dirt-dauber said
    There is no woman here

But the head saw the impression of her body
on the earth
    I see the print of her body
    he said
    I even see the print of her cunt

The dirt-dauber said
    Well then look for her

The head went in the house
and saw only two men
on each side of the house a man
sleeping

He looked at the man who had been a woman
    I wonder he said I wonder
    if this man can pee as high as the house

So the dirt-dauber said to the man who had been the young wife
    Well
       let him see if you can do that

They went outside the head watched intently
and she who had been a woman and was now a man
pissed clear over the roof

Then they went back in the house
and the head went to the other
his brother disguised and
made him do likewise and
watched intently

But the other his brother
could only pee half as high
which made the head laugh
and laugh

Then the head put four pottery pots in
a row
four in a row
and he said to the man who had been the young woman
    Can you shoot an arrow through all those

So the dirt-dauber said to the man
who had been the woman
    Well
       let him see if you can do that

She the man who had been the woman
shot an arrow
into the four pottery pots
the four all in a row
and the arrow went through all of them

The head said to the other man
    Do the same thing

And the dirt-dauber said
    Well
    let him see if you can do it

But when this man really a man
shot his arrow it went into
only one
only one and stopped
and the head laughed and laughed

So then the head said
to the man who had been a woman
    Let me see if you can go hunting and kill something

And the dirt-dauber said
    Well
    let him see you do that

So the woman went hunting
while the head flew along watching
watching

She killed a deer
the head examined it all over and said
    Kill something else

She killed another deer
the head examined it all over and said
    Never mind

Now they came to a stream and
the man who had been a woman
swam into the stream
so did the head

But the man who had been a woman
dived under the water
and said something magic
    something magic

And then she said to the head
    Now this will be your home

And she turned back into a woman
and swam to the bank of the stream and
ran away laughing

while the head tumbled
               and tumbled
                     and tumbled
in the water

and could never get out

Adapted from a tale in John R. Swanton, *Myths and Tales of the Southeastern Indians, BAE Bulletin 88,* Washington, D.C., 1929. The story was told by Watt Sam, one of the few remaining speakers of the Natchez tongue when Swanton knew him near Braggs, Oklahoma, between the years 1908 and 1914. Swanton writes that Watt Sam told him this story of the Rolling Head "must be told only during cold weather. Otherwise bad luck would follow."

NATCHEZ: *The Corn Mother and Her Son*

Old Corn-Woman lived with a certain boy

Whenever she was out of corn she went to the corn house and
when she came back she always brought a basket full of corn

One time the boy looked into the corn house and saw nothing
    there

        (Where does she get the corn?)
        (The next time I will watch her)

The next time she went in the corn house he watched
peeking through a crack

There she sat astride a basket
    she shook herself and made a noise
        and the basket was instantly filled

        (What she does is shit in the basket!)
        (I will not eat that hominy!)

So the boy refused to eat and when he would not eat
the Corn Mother knew he had seen her

    Since you think I am dirty go to your kinfolks
        your grandmother
        your aunt
        your two uncles
        your elder brother
        your sister

                    your other mother
                    your father

        I took you from them but if you think I am filthy
        you go back
        But first you must kill me and burn down my house
        before you go away

        But before you do any of that
        go and hunt some birds

The boy went out killing birds and brought them in
kind after kind
chickadees and topknot birds
and parrakeets and blue jays

When he brought blue jays and parrakeets
        These are the ones (she said)

Then she brought all the birds to life she
put the parrakeets and the blue jays on his shoulders and
all the other birds all over him chickadees
on the top of his head
topknot birds on his back
other birds at his belt

And she made a flute for him

when he played it all the birds sang

        Now when you go away (she said) you will meet
        at a crossroad some women some bad women
        they will ask you to lie with them

        You must not do that
        they will have teeth in their cunts teeth
        that could cut off your penis

You will meet three of these women and then another one

the first three you will refuse but
with the last one you will lie down but

turn your penis into stone before you
put it inside her

Then the boy killed Corn-Woman and burned the house down
down to a bed of coals
as she had told him to do

Then he started off walking away

he went along blowing on his flute

the birds were singing

When there at a crossroad a woman waited
    Fuck me won't you please (she said)

but he refused

Then appeared the second woman
    Put your cock in me (she said)

and again he refused

The third woman met him and asked him
and again he refused

When then the fourth woman stood by the trail
    Fuck me won't you now (she said)
and he said yes and lay down with her

Then he turned his penis to stone and
pushed it inside her and broke the teeth in her cunt

And she lay there crying

Based on John R. Swanton, *Myths and Tales of the Southeastern Indians, BAE Bulletin 88,* Washington, D.C., 1929. "The motive of the vagina dentata," he writes, "is widely spread, occurring among the Bella-coola, Shuswap, Chilcotin, Kwakiutl, Newettee, Comox, Tsimshian, Utamqt, Thompson, Shoshoni, Dakota, Arapaho, Pawnee, Maidu, Wichita, Jicarilla, Chuckchee (in Siberia), Ainu (in Japan). . . ."

PAIUTE: *Ghost Dance Song*

The whirlwind! The whirlwind!

The new earth comes into being
         swiftly as snow.

The new earth comes into being
         quietly as snow.

Adapted from James Mooney, "The Ghost Dance Re-
ligion . . ." in *Fourteenth Annual BAE Report,* Wash-
ington, D.C., 1896.

QEE'ESH: CALENDAR: *Fragments*

April   The first month of the year
the month when the rain has come and the grass is
       sprouting
when the grass begins to grow green

      The spiderweb now catches butterflies and grass-
        hoppers

June   Now the eagles fly

      In this month the young eagles first fly

August   The brown month

      In this month all is seared and brown

October   Now the little winds whistle
winds through the leafless trees
fallen leaves in the streams of water

      This is the month of mist

December   The month of fatness
the bear sheds his hair and says
      I am fat
the whale now is fat

      In this month the deer grows fat

February   The month of leafing trees
the season of sprouting

when snakes crawl forth and frogs sing

Trees awaken and put out leaves

From Constance Goddard DuBois, *The Religion of the Luiseño Indians of Southern California,* University of California Publications in American Archaeology and Ethnology, Vol. 8, No. 3, 1908. Qee'esh was the tribal name of a group of Indians gathered at San Luis Rey Mission.

WINTU: *The North Star*

The stars streaming in the sky are my hair
The round rim of the earth which you see
Binds my starry hair

Adapted from Jeremiah Curtin, *Creation Myths of Primitive America*, Boston, 1898.

History of Nez Perce Indians from 1805 up to the Present Time 1880 by James Reuben, Nez Perce Indian

They lived and enjoyed the happiness and freedom
and lived just as happy as any other Nation in the World.

But alas the day was coming when all their happy days
was to be turned into day of sorrow and moening.

Their days of freedom was turned to be the day of slavery.

Their days of victory was turned to be conquered,
and their rights to the country was disregarded by another nations
which is called "Whiteman" at present day.

In 1855 a treaty was made between Nez Perce Nation and United
      States.

Wal-la-mot-kin (Hair tied on forehead) or Old Joseph,
Hul-lal-ho-sot or (Lawyer),
were the two leading Chiefs of the Nez Perce Nation in 1855,
both of these two Chiefs consented to the treaty
and Nez Perce sold to the United States
part of their country.

In 1863 another treaty was made
in which Lawyer and his people consented
but Joseph and his people refused to make the second treaty

from that time Joseph's people
were called None-treaty Nez Perce.

The treaty Nez Perce number 1800

None-treaty numbered 1000

The Nez Perse decreased greatly since 1805 up to 1863.
The smallpox prevailed among the tribe
which almost destroyed the tribe.

Lawyer's people advanced in civilization
and became farmers ec.
They had their children in schools.

While Joseph's people refused all these things
they lived outside what was called Nez Perce Reservation

1877 Government undertook to move Young Joseph people on
the Res.

At this date Young Joseph was the ruling chief
son of Old Chief Joseph who died in 1868,
and left his people in charge of his own Son

Joseph and his followers broke out
and there was Nez Perce War bloody one
nine great battles fought

the last battle lasted five days
which Joseph surrendered with his people

1000 Indians had went on the war path
but when Joseph surrendered
there was only 600

400 killed during the wars
or went to other tribes.

after the capture Joseph was brought to this Territory as captives.

at present Joseph people numbers 350 out of 600
all are suffering on account of this Southern climate
result is he and his people
will live and die in this country exiled from home

Take it in the right light—
Nez Perce have been wrongly treated by the Government
it cannot be denied
not Nez Perce only but all other Indian Nations in America.

I wrote this about my own people.

I am a member of Nez Perce Tribe
and Nephew of Chief Joseph

When this is opened and read may be understood
how the Indians have been treated by the Whiteman.

Slightly abridged from the text by James Reuben deposited in the cornerstone of the Nez Percé and Ponca school on October 20, 1880, and recovered when the schoolhouse was torn down. It was first printed by the Oklahoma Historical Society in the *Chronicles of Oklahoma,* Vol. 12, September, 1934.

NEZ PERCE: *Guardian-spirit Song*

Ravening Coyote comes
red hands
red mouth
necklace of eye-balls!

From Spinden, *Songs of the Tewa*, New York, 1933.

KWAKIUTL: *Potlatch Boasts*

Do not let our chief rise too high
Do not let him destroy too much property
else we shall be made like broken pieces of copper by the
    great breaker of coppers
    the great splitter of coppers
    the great chief who throws coppers into the water
    the great one who can not be surpassed by anybody
    the one surmounting all the chiefs

                       (Sung by the rival chief in reply) :

What will my rival say again
that spider woman
what will he pretend to do next?
The words of that spider woman do not go a straight way
Will he not brag that he is going to give canoes
that he is going to break coppers
that he is going to give a grease feast?

Do you know what you will be like?
You will be like an old dog
you will spread your legs before me when I get excited
You did so when I broke the great coppers "Cloud" and "Making
    Ashamed"
    my great property
    and the great coppers "Chief" and "Killer Whale"
    and the one named "Point of Island"

and "The Feared One" and "Beaver"
This I throw into your face

Adapted from Franz Boas, "The Ethnology of the Kwakiutl, based on Data Collected by George Hunt," *Thirty-fifth Annual BAE Report,* Washington, D.C., 1921.

TLINGIT: *Mourning Song for a Brother Drowned at Sea*

perhaps he went into the sun's trail

                  so that I can never see him again

From John R. Swanton, *Tlingit Myths and Texts, BAE Bulletin 39,* Washington, D.C., 1909.

ESKIMO: *Spring Song, Fragment*

Glorious it is
To see young women
Gathering in little groups
And paying visits in the houses—
Then all at once the men
Do so want to be manly. . . .

. . . Glorious it is
To see long haired winter caribou
Returning to the forests . . .
. . . While the herd follows the ebb-mark of the sea
With a storm of clattering hooves.
Glorious it is
When wandering time is come.

From Knud Rasmussen, *The Intellectual Culture of the Iglulik Eskimos,* Copenhagen, 1929.

ESKIMO: *Song, Fragment*

The lands around my dwelling are
now more beautiful
from the day when
it is given me to see
faces I have never seen before

From an impromptu song sung by an Eskimo woman
to her guests, a party of European travelers, one of
whom was Knud Rasmussen, greatest of interpreters
of the Eskimo mind and poetry; reprinted here from
the English translation by W. J. Worster of Knud Ras-
mussen's Danish in *The Intellectual Culture of the
Iglulik Eskimos*. Report of the Fifth Thule Expedition,
1921-24, Copenhagen, 1929.

POSTFACE: *The Sources*

There are thousands of volumes of raw material, although very few are neat collections of readable poetry. Most are cold-eyed cumbersome reports: religious, military, scientific, with only here and there a quoted echo of "savage" poetry gleaming through.

Nahuatl (the language of the Toltecs, the Aztecs and some of their neighbors) literature alone includes hundreds of sixteenth-century manuscripts and countless subsequent studies. The best survey of this vast array is, so far as I know, still untranslated from the Spanish, the two-volume *Historia de la Literatura Nahuatl* (Mexico, 1953-54) by Angel Maria Garibay K. [intana], the principal modern authority. The best survey available in English translation is Miguel Leon-Portilla, *Aztec Thought and Culture* (Norman, Okla., 1963). An impressive single work easily accessible in English is the *General History of the Things of New Spain,* the *Florentine Codex,* translated from the Aztec in the sixteenth century by Fray Bernardino de Sahagun, now in a new English translation by Charles E. Dibble and Arthur J. O. Anderson, published in thirteen volumes as Monograph No. 14 of the School of American Research (Santa Fe, 1950 ff.).

Collections of Maya literature, chiefly post-Spanish fragments of history, prophecy, dismembered liturgy, and commentaries thereon, are less plentiful. I have drawn on three such collections in this book: Maud W. Makemson, *The Book of the Jaguar Priest: A Translation of the Book of Chilam Balam of Tizimin, with Commentary* (New York, 1951); Ralph L. Roys, *The Book of Chilam Balam of Chumayel* (Washington, 1933); and *Popol Vuh: the Sacred Book of the Ancient Quiché Maya,* translated into Spanish by Adrian Recinos and into English by Sylvanus G. Morley and Delia Goetz (Norman, 1950). There are more than a dozen other Chilam Balam collections, several in translations by Roys, who has most recently done the superb *Ritual of the Bacabs* (Norman, 1965), a collection of Mayan medical incantations. An unusual book by Gertrude Prokosch Kurath and Samuel Marti, *Dances of Anáhuac: The Choreography and Music of Precortesian Dances* (Viking Publication No. 38, 1964), gives an idea of what can be read of the songs, dances, religion and philosophy of the Nahuas and Mayas by a careful study of sculptures and inscriptions as well as of manuscripts and picture writing.

The basic collections of texts for North America in general are found in the publications of the Bureau of American Ethnology, Smithsonian Institution: the *Annual BAE Reports,* from 1 to 48 (Washington, 1881-1933); *BAE Bulletins* (Washington, 1887 to date); and, especially in the earlier years, occasional *Introductions, Miscellaneous Publications,* and *Contributions.* Various of the *Reports* and the *Bulletins* contain collections of songs and tales and poems that are fundamental to the North American literature, particularly the several such items by Francis La Flesche, John R. Swanton, and Frances Densmore, the greatest song hunter of all. One of the more beautiful BAE collections is that in the *Twenty-second Annual Report* (Washington, 1904) on the Hako, a Pawnee ceremony, by Alice C. Fletcher and James R. Murie with the assistance of Tahirussawichi, an aged Pawnee priest; another is the handful of songs in literal translation accompanying the article on the Pima by Frank Russell in the *Twenty-sixth Annual Report* (Washington, 1908); another, a little gallery of veritable masterpieces, is *BAE Bulletin 98, Tales of the Cochiti Indians* (1931), collected by Ruth Benedict. There are many more.

The same Ruth Benedict's two-volume *Zuñi Mythology* is Vol. 21 of *Columbia University Contributions to Anthropology.* Scholarly programs of publications in ethnology have nearly all included important collections of tales or songs or ceremonies, such as A. L. Kroeber's *Gros Ventre Myths and Tales* in Vol. 1 (1907) of the *Anthropological Papers of the American Museum of Natural History;* or Washington Matthews' *Navaho Myths, Prayers and Songs, with texts and translations,* Vol. 5, No. 2 (Berkeley, 1907) of *University of California Publications in American Archaeology and Ethnology,* to name only a couple of rather early items from the enormous total of such titles.

Numerous periodicals in and about the precincts of ethnology have published native American literature, a few by the bale, most by the scrap: *American Anthropologist;* the *Journal of American Ethnology and Archaeology;* the *International Journal of Linguistics; American Quarterly Register and Magazine,* "The Ancient Cherokee Traditions and Religious Rites" in Vol. 3 (December 1849); *Therapeutic Gazette* has James Mooney's "The Mescal Plant Ceremony" in Vol. 12, 3rd Series, (1896), for a few examples past and present. The *Journal of American Folklore* has from its inception regularly published Indian pieces; Franz Boas' "On Certain Songs and Dances of the Kwakiutl" and his "Chinook Songs" appeared in Vol. 1 in 1888. Volumes 27 (1914) and 34 (1921) contain bibliographies of these earlier Indian items.

Each region and each period has its specialists, whose individual bibliographies might run to many pages, such as Washington Matthews among the Navajo nearly a hundred years ago or Father Berard Haile and Leland C. Wyman, together and separately, in recent works of Navajo literature—their *Beautyway* (New York, 1957), for one elegant example.

General collections have been appearing for centuries but became epidemic in the United States during the late nineteenth century and the early 1900's, nearly always with either scientific or Cub Scout overtones, seldom presented as serious literature. One resounding exception is Daniel G. Brinton's eight-volume *Library of American Aboriginal Literature* (Philadelphia, 1882–90), including works from the Delaware, Iroquois, Creek, Nahuatl, and Maya. The translations are old-fashioned but still magnificent, as could for that matter be said of the codification of Homer put in written form by Pisistratus. A small collection of poems containing, in its Introduction, a discussion of Indian literature that is serious, scholarly, and yet marvelously apt and reasonable (only a little disfigured by the pseudo-scientific view of "primitive" singing for "power"—what the hell did Milton sing for?—that deforms nearly all such present-day discussions) is *Songs of the Tewa* (New York, 1933) by Herbert J. Spinden. Somewhat more recent collections are Margot Astrov, *The Winged Serpent: American Indian Prose and Poetry* (New York, 1945), and A. Grove Day, *The Sky Clears: Poetry of the American Indian* (New York, 1951). American Indian and Eskimo selections are included in Willard R. Trask's two-volume worldwide anthology, *The Unwritten Song* (New York, 1966), and in Jerome Rothenberg, *Technicians of the Sacred* (New York, 1968), an anthology principally of ceremonial poetry, much of it dazzling, from around the world.